MARIO AND LUIGI:

SUPER MARIO BROS HEROES

x1983

Kenny Abdo

Fly!
An Imprint of Abdo Zoom
abdobooks.com

abdobooks.com

Published by Abdo Zoom, a division of ABDO, P.O. Box 398166, Minneapolis, Minnesota 55439. Copyright © 2021 by Abdo Consulting Group, Inc. International copyrights reserved in all countries. No part of this book may be reproduced in any form without written permission from the publisher. Fly!™ is a trademark and logo of Abdo Zoom.

Printed in the United States of America, North Mankato, Minnesota.
052020
092020

♻ THIS BOOK CONTAINS
RECYCLED MATERIALS

Photo Credits: Alamy, Everette Collection, Flickr, Getty Images, iStock, Newscom, Pond5, Shuttertock, ©Jullienne p.6 / CC BY-NC-ND 2.0, ©Daniel Costa p.6, 10, 11 CC BY-NC-ND 2.0, ©Ricardo Saramago p.7 / CC BY-NC-ND 2.0, ©Philroc p.9 / CC BY-SA 4.0, ©BagoGames p.18 / CC BY 2.0
Production Contributors: Kenny Abdo, Jennie Forsberg, Grace Hansen
Design Contributors: Dorothy Toth, Neil Klinepier

Library of Congress Control Number: 2019956165

Publisher's Cataloging-in-Publication Data

Names: Abdo, Kenny, author.
Title: Mario and Luigi: Super Mario Bros heroes / by Kenny Abdo
Other title: Super Mario Bros heroes
Description: Minneapolis, Minnesota : Abdo Zoom, 2021 | Series: Video game heroes | Includes online resources and index.
Identifiers: ISBN 9781098221461 (lib. bdg.) | ISBN 9781644944202 (pbk.) | ISBN 9781098222444 (ebook) | ISBN 9781098222932 (Read-to-Me ebook)
Subjects: LCSH: Video game characters--Juvenile literature. | Super Mario Bros. (Game)--Juvenile literature. | Nintendo video games--Juvenile literature. | Heroes -Juvenile literature.
Classification: DDC 794.8--dc23

TABLE OF CONTENTS

Mario & Luigi 4

Player Profile 8

Level Up 12

Expansion Pack 18

Glossary 22

Online Resources 23

Index 24

MARIO & LUIGI

Wrecking **goombas** and rescuing princesses, the Mario Brothers are two heroes who can save the day and fix your faulty toilet!

Mario and Luigi are the most famous characters in video game history. Mario alone has appeared in more than 200 video games.

PLAYER PROFILE

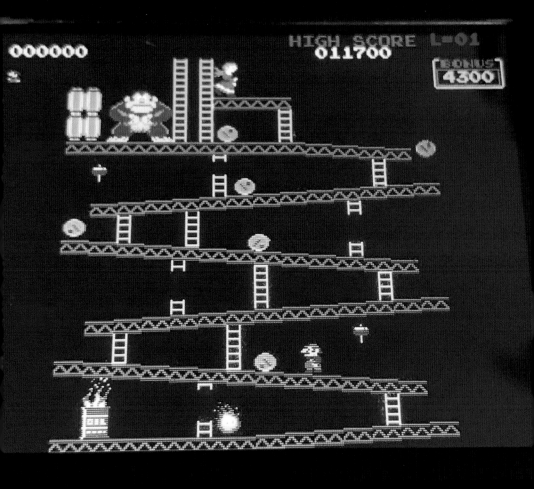

Mario was created by Shigeru
Miyamoto. He was first seen in
the video game *Donkey Kong* in
1981. Although then, his name was
Jumpman. He was a carpenter in
Donkey Kong, not a plumber.

Mario was named after Mario Segale. He was the **landlord** of Nintendo of America's office. Miyamoto was inspired when Segale barged in on a meeting demanding overdue rent.

Miyamoto got Luigi's name from a pizza parlour called Mario & Luigi's. *Ruiji* means "similar" in Japanese. Miyamoto felt that was appropriate because Luigi and Mario are so similar.

LEVEL UP

Luigi was finally introduced in 1983 in the *Mario Bros.* **arcade** game. The game took place in the New York City sewer system.

Super Mario Bros. came out on the Nintendo Entertainment System (NES) in 1985. It was a massive hit. It sold more than 40 million copies!

MARIO
000000 ▌×00

WORLD TIME
1-1

SUPER
MARIO BROS.™

©1985 1993 NINTENDO

●1 PLAYER GAME

TOP- 134850

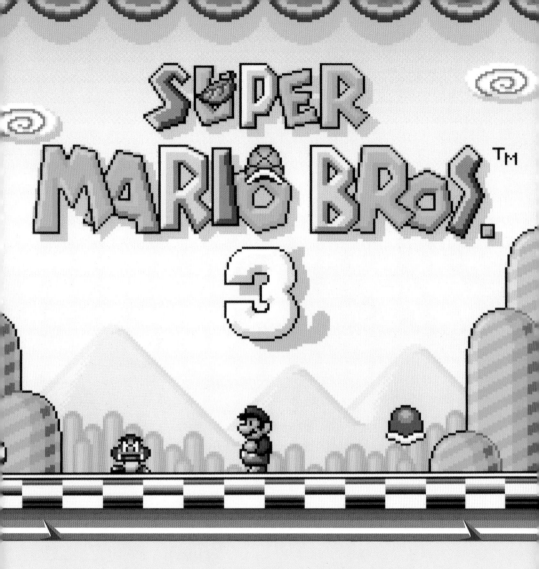

Super Mario Bros. 2 and *3* were
released soon after. The games
introduced **iconic** characters like
Princess Peach and Toad. Lovable
Yoshi made his **debut** in 1990's *Super
Mario World*. This game was released
for the very popular Super NES.

Mario made his 3D **debut** in the revolutionary *Super Mario 64*. He had to once again defeat the evil King Koopa, while saving Princess Peach and the Mushroom Kingdom.

Since then, Mario and Luigi have jumped from the Nintendo Game Cube, to the Wii, to the Switch. Each game gives our two favorite heroes more awesome adventures!

EXPANSION PACK

Mario and Luigi have enjoyed many careers throughout several games over the years. They have been doctors, pro tennis players, and ghost hunters, to name a few.

Mario and Luigi made the leap onto big and small screens. In 1989, *The Super Mario Bros. Super Show!* premiered. In 1993, the live-action movie, *Super Mario Bros.*, was released.

The Super Mario Bros. series is in the *Guinness Book of World Records* as the most successful gaming **franchise** of all time. The Mario Bros aren't just super entertaining, but super popular too!

GLOSSARY

arcade – an indoor space that has multiple video games to play.

debut – a first appearance.

franchise – a collection of related video games in a series.

goomba – the first enemies faced in the *Mario Bros.* franchise. They are walking mushrooms.

iconic – commonly known for its excellence.

landlord – a person who owns or runs houses, apartments, or buildings and rents them to other people.

ONLINE RESOURCES

Booklinks
NONFICTION NETWORK
FREE! ONLINE NONFICTION RESOURCES

To learn more about Mario & Luigi, please visit **abdobooklinks.com** or scan this QR code. These links are routinely monitored and updated to provide the most current information available.

INDEX

Donkey Kong (game) 9

gaming systems 12, 14, 15, 17

Guinness Book of World Records 21

Mario Bros. (game) 12

Miyamoto, Shigeru 9, 10, 11

Princess Peach (character) 15

Segale, Mario 10

Super Mario 64 (game) 16

Super Mario Bros. (game) 14

Super Mario Bros. (movie) 20

Super Mario Bros. 2 (game) 15

Super Mario Bros. 3 (game) 15

Super Mario Bros. Super Show!
(TV show) 20

Toad (character) 15

Yoshi (character) 15